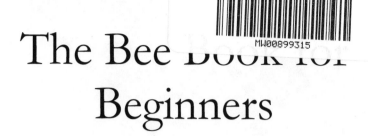

The Bee Book for
Beginners

Second Edition (Revised)

An Apiculture Starter

Or

How to Be a Backyard Beekeeper

And

Harvest Honey from Your Own Bee Hives

Frank Randall

@BackyardFarmBks
facebook.com/BackyardFarmBooks
backyardfarmbooks.com

ISBN: 1479298034
ISBN-13: 978-1479298037

DEDICATION

To backyard owners everywhere -
whether a farmer in your heart or just your dreams.

CONTENTS

INTRODUCTION

If you have a taste for honey or an adventurous side, maybe you have thought of becoming a beekeeper. What would you really be in for, though? Is it really a job or is it a fun way to get your own honey? Well, it's really both.

Being a beekeeper is a lot of work, but it also has a lot of benefits. Anyone can do it, as long as they are prepared. You can't just wake up one day, decide to be a beekeeper and start immediately. You have to know what you are doing.

That's why I have written this book. Within its pages, you'll discover the tools you need to be a beekeeper, what to expect from your hive, how to harvest your honey, and how to protect the hive from various problems and invaders. I'll teach you what types of bees are best to keep, the jobs of each bee in the hive, how to choose and position your hives, and more.

When I started keeping bees, I spent a lot of time and money on a lot of books before I was sure that apiculture was going to be a part of my life.

This easy to read beginner's book summarizes the essential information I have learned over the years and is written to help you decide if beekeeping really is for you.

Best wishes,

Frank

Frank Randall

1

BEE BIOLOGY 101

If you want to be a beekeeper, one of the most important steps is learning to recognize each type of bee in your hive: the workers, the drones, and the queen. Not only that, but you need to have an understanding of how each type of bee comes into existence and how to tell when your colony might be having any problems. Luckily, most of that is easy to understand.

The Queen's Job

The queen is the ruler of the honeybee hive. Her primary job is to lay eggs and keep the hive going. The other female bees, the workers, ensure that their queen is well fed and cared for. Amazingly, a queen bee can lay her own body weight in eggs in a single day. That's up to 2,000 eggs in only 24 hours!

Raising, Recognizing and Marking a Queen

The worker bees determine which cells will be queen cells. A queen cell is larger than a worker cell, and the larvae in a queen cell eats royal jelly. After a while, the larva turns into a pupa. Then, the pupa turns into the adult queen bee. That entire process usually takes about 16 days.

It's easy to recognize a queen after she emerges from the incubation cell. Like the workers she will have a stinger but she won't have any pollen collection "baskets" on her legs. Also, queen bees are larger than workers and have an elongated abdomen.

However, even with those differences, it can be difficult to find your queen amongst the other bees in the hive. You can buy marked queens to easily spot them in the hive. Or you can carefully mark them yourself. Just buy a bee-marking pen from a bee product distributor and use it to put a small dot on your queen. Be sure to do it in spring or summer, when the hive is small and there's less chance of a swarm. Also, don't forget to use a smoker to calm the hive down first.

The Queen's Mating Process

Once the queen emerges from the incubation cell, the first part of her job begins. She must mate with the sexually mature male bees, the drones. Although the drones will occasionally leave the hive to stretch their wings during non-mating times, the queen will usually only leave the hive to mate.

The queen's mating flight is sometimes known as the "nuptial flight." In that single flight, the queen can mate with up to 20 drones. She also has the ability to store that sperm indefinitely within her body. Because of this, a fertilized queen can supply eggs for the hive easily throughout her life.

The Queen's Life Span

Some queen bees have been known to live for up to six years, but on average live for one to two years. The exact life span of the queen is determined by a number of factors including the location and health of the hive. As a beekeeper, it will be your job to properly maintain your hive and to watch out for any signs of illness.

Replacing the Queen

The queen bee produces certain pheromones and other indicators that will alert the worker bees to her health status. Any time the queen is judged to be too old, ill, or somehow incapacitated, the workers will ensure that a potential substitute is born. The queen must then defend her title, which in many cases can mean a fight to the death.

If you, as a beekeeper, sense that your queen is in trouble, you also have the option to replace the queen yourself by buying a successor queen. However, in most cases it's best to just let your bees work out their own problems. Too much interference with the hive dynamic can often lead to more problems.

The Life of a Drone

There can be up to several hundred drone bees in a given hive. Drone bee larvae are fed royal jelly and come out of incubation cells that are just a touch larger than worker bee cells, after about 24 days. Drones are born without stingers and never develop them. In addition, they are easy to recognize because of their huge eyes and extra antennae segments.

At first glance, drone bees seem to have a fabulous life. They aren't responsible for collecting nectar, storing honey, caring for the queen, or any other hive functions. They can simply sit back, relax, and let the worker bees do all the work, including keeping the drones healthy and ready for mating.

But while the drones might seem like kings with servants, they have a fairly bad lot in life. As soon as they mate with the queen, they die. Those that don't mate with the queen get kicked out of the hive by the drones in the fall.

Drone bees that are kicked out of the hive have to fend for themselves. With winter coming on, they quickly die off. Therefore, no matter what, a drone bee is doomed from the start.

The Life of a Worker

Worker bees do almost everything in a hive. That's why about 95 percent of a hive is made up of workers and only five percent is made up of drones.

Worker bees generally gestate for about 21 days. When they emerge, they quickly start to take on the jobs of the hive, such as collecting nectar, producing honey and royal jelly, tending to the young larvae as well as the queen, determining how many of each new incubation cell is needed at any time, and keeping the unsuspecting drones fed and happy.

If a population gets too large for a hive, the worker bees will even determine when it is time to split off into other colonies. That's called swarming. As a beekeeper, part of your job is controlling swarming by making sure that your bees have plenty of space. If a colony needs to be split, it's better to recognize it yourself.

Beekeeping isn't always easy, but it's always interesting. As long as you watch your hive and get to know it, you should be able to recognize any problems early on. Your bees will generally take care of themselves, but they may need your intervention from time to time. Just take your basic knowledge of bee biology and apply it to the situation at hand.

2

HOW LONG HAS BEEKEEPING BEEN POPULAR?

If you're interested in becoming a beekeeper, you are probably wondering a bit about the history of beekeeping and how long it has been a popular practice. Well, that depends on how you define the term "beekeeping."

Bee and Honey Hunting

The history of modern-day beekeeping methods has its roots in the ancient practice of bee and honey hunting. As far back as 10,000 years ago, humans went in search of honey. There are even cave paintings in Egypt, Europe, and other areas of the bee hunting practices of the time.

Bee colonies would usually be found in hollowed out trees and logs. Once found, the hunter took what he wanted, leaving the hive destroyed. There was no such things as extraction devices or co-existing with and caring for a bee colony.

Bee hunting still exists today. Families who live in woodsy areas of the United States, for example, often go out in search of honey. Hunting for honey is also still practiced in India, where modern day hunters gather honey from the *Apis dorsata*, or giant honey bee. In fact, India has a rich history of bee hunting. When ancient residents of India were living in forests and caves, they thought of honey as a gift from their god. As they became more civilized, honey was considered a type of magic potion. Some of the things that the Indian culture attributed to honey were:

o Fertile land
o Bountiful crops
o Thriving cattle
o Female fertility

Obviously all of those beliefs led to a boom in bee hunting and, later, to the domestication of bees.

Domestication versus Modern-Day Beekeeping

Domestication of bees, which has its roots in Europe and Asia, is not the same thing as modern-day beekeeping. Bee domestication simply means encouraging bees to take up residence nearby for the purpose of collecting their honey.

Romans, Egyptians and Israelites domesticated bees by encouraging them to live in hollow logs, pots, and wooden boxes. There are references in the bible and the works of the Roman writer Virgil of early people in many other parts of the world doing the same thing.

It wasn't until the late 18th century that Thomas Wilding first proposed that bees didn't need to be killed in order to harvest their honey. Prior to that, domesticated bees were kept until the honey was ready and then hives were destroyed during harvesting.

The Father of American Beekeeping

The Reverend Lorenzo Lorraine Langstroth, who is known as the Father of American Apiculture, was born in 1810. By the time he died in 1895, he had revolutionized the way that people looked at beekeeping or honey hunting through the creation of the Langstroth hive design, which was based on the work of another famous bee researcher, Francois Huber.

Huber discovered that bees designed their hives to have specific functions based on the space allocated. Langstroth then noted that when his bees had less than 3/8 inch of available space to move around in, they would neither build comb into that space nor cement it closed with propolis, a substance used to fill in gaps elsewhere in the hive. He called those areas "bee space."

Langstroth later took that discovery one step further and calculated that the bee space was specifically 1/4 to 3/8 of an inch. Langstroth designed a new form of hive based on those measurements. He found out that the bees would build their honeycombs with enough space between each that the honeycombs could be easily removed from the hive and then put back later on. That meant that people could actually learn to co-exist with their bees and keep the hive alive, while still getting their valuable honey and beeswax.

His book, *Langstroth on the Hive and Honey-bee*, published in 1853, described his observation of the bee space and illustrated his patented hive, which had removable frames. That hive design is still used in many parts of the world today.

Hybridization and the "Bee Boom"

The invention of the Langstroth hive meant that more people got into the beekeeping world not just for their own family to have the honey but also for business reasons. So, modern beekeeping was born, which quickly led to the idea of bee hybridization and specific breeding. Bees were soon bred to produce more honey and to be more resilient. Hives began to live longer and be more resistant to diseases, changing weather, and other problems of the past.

Symbiotic Relationships

The "bee boom" in North America and Europe led to beekeepers designing entire areas just for their bees. In fact, many people started to combine growing their own food and flowers with keeping their bees healthy and happy. The fact that all of the flowering plants were right there handy kept the bees happy. In fact, beekeepers even started including shallow water sources in their garden designs, just for the bees.

A symbiotic relationship developed between bees and their keepers. The keepers cared for the bees and, in exchange, the bees produced honey and beeswax for the keepers. Many keepers adopted the idea of taking only what they needed and making sure that their hives had enough materials left over to sustain the hive through the winter.

Modern Beekeeping Technology

As the symbiotic relationship between bees and their keepers grew, so did modern beekeeping technology. These days, electric honey extractors, heated bee houses, various types of smokers, hive tools, and modern beekeeping protective gear all keep evolving, making the honey harvesting process easier on both the keepers and the bees.

The relationship between man and bee goes back thousands of years so as you use your hive tool to open up and inspect your hive, remember that you are in good company. Reflecting on all the innovative beekeepers that have come before you might lead you on to create your own beekeeping innovations and make your own beekeeping discoveries. Even if you're not the innovative type, you can't help but "bee" inspired by the many wonderful things about modern bees and their hives.

3

WHAT DOES A BEE DO ALL DAY?

If you want to be a beekeeper, it's important to understand what your bees do all day, which can vary day to day, depending on the type of bee and its stage of development. Even though worker bees make up about 95 percent of the hive, understanding the queen and the drones is also vital. Every member of a hive has a role to play and gets some rewards.

The Queen Bee

What the queen bee does all day depends a bit on what day it is. For example, on the first day that the queen emerges from her incubation cell (egg) she doesn't necessarily just take over ruling the hive. It's possible that another queen might already be present and there can only be one hive ruler.

Unfortunately, queen bees don't really have the ability to flip a coin or diplomatically agree on who will rule the honeybee hive. So they have to resort to violence. A new queen will often get into a duel to the death with the reigning queen.

The good news for the new queen is that the odds are usually in her favor. Worker bees have the ability to tell when a reigning queen is too old or somehow unable to rule. That's when they create a new queen bee incubation cell. So, if the workers have "read" their queen properly, the new queen's job of taking over should be fairly easy.

Soon after taking over the hive, the queen bee will go on a nuptial flight and mate with a bunch of the drones. Sometimes she'll mate with 20 or more drones in that flight. Then her real job will begin.

When the nuptial flight is over, the queen bee will hunker down in the hive, where she'll most likely live out her life without seeing the outside world again. Except, of course, when the light comes streaming in during your hive inspections. All she will do is stay in the egg laying chamber and lay eggs. That's it. The worker bees will feed and care for her and her daily activities will be quite boring from then on out until the next queen arrives to take over.

Drones

The daily life of a drone is just about as mundane and boring as the queen's daily life. Drones are fed and cared for by the worker bees. They don't need to do any of the hive chores or go out and harvest nectar. Although some drones opt to leave the nest to stretch their wings now and then. The only time you might witness a drone bee having a busy day is if he is mating with the queen or if the workers kick him out of the hive. If you witness such a thing, you should get ready to pay your last respects because drones die right after they mate with the queen. Any drones that don't mate with her are kicked out of the hive in the fall and also tend to die quickly. Suddenly, the mundane daily life of a drone sounds a lot better than the task of mating, doesn't it? That's why a good beekeeper knows to have some respect for the poor little drone bees.

Workers

The worker bees do practically everything within a beehive.
The daily life of a worker bee depends a lot on the age of that worker. Think of it as getting an entry-level job at the start of your career and then progressing up to higher positions. The same thing happens in a honeybee hive.

Starter Jobs

When a worker bee is young it can have several starter jobs. Usually day one and two is when they clean out the brood cells, or incubation cells, which prepares them for the next egg. Once the cells are clean, the worker bees turn into nurses, feeding all incubating larva. They are usually nurses from about day 3 to 11.

The Wax Production Phase

From day 12 to 17 the worker bee's body can produce wax from between its abdomen segments, during the wax production phase. The worker bee uses the wax to repair old cells, build new ones, and securely store away pollen and nectar, which is harvested by other workers. It's a busy time for worker bees, but most times are busy in their own ways.

Delegation of Tasks

From day 18 to 21 there is a certain delegation of tasks that takes place within the hive. A worker bee that happens to be in between jobs might be tasked with attending to the queen, ventilating the hives with propolis, fanning the hive, gathering water to add in the fanning and cooling process, or even disposing of dead bees.

So, mortuary bees have a very important position. They have to carry larvae that didn't hatch properly and dead bees well away from the hive. The dead bee disposal process is especially important because it helps to prevent disease from taking over within the hive.

Foraging

From day 22 to 42 of its life, a worker bee is likely to be a forager. Its job will be to go out and gather propolis, pollen, and nectar for the hive that it stores in "baskets" called corbicula on its legs. A foraging bee can travel up to a mile and a half away from the hive in a given day.

Hive Protection

Finally, one of the most important daily tasks of a worker bee is as a hive protector. Drones don't have stingers. So, the workers must fend off any invading animals or humans. Of course, as a beekeeper, you can rest easy when you inspect your hives, as long as you use a smoker and the right protective gear.

4

HOW DO I CHOOSE THE LOCATION OF MY HIVE?

Beekeepers refer to finding a hive location as "siting." If you are siting a hive, you really have to understand your bees, your land, yourself, your family, your neighbors, and a lot of other factors, including weather patterns. So here are some tips for properly siting your hive.

Consider the Law

Just because you own the land doesn't mean you necessarily have a right to put in a beehive. Some towns and cities have ordinances against it. So, it's important to familiarize yourself with the local laws before you actually choose a hive location. That will save you from dealing with the headache of paying fines, relocating your hives, or even going to jail!

Consider the Sun

Although bees like some sunlight, you don't want to bake your bees. The general rule is that bees like early morning sun, followed by shade, and then a little bit of late afternoon or early evening sun. If you don't have such a spot on your property, try making one. You can plant some shade trees or use other means to adjust the environment around the hive to create the ideal conditions for your bees. Also, it can give you a lot more hive placement options.

Another suggestion is to find someone nearby with a lot of land and ask them if you can keep bees on a corner of their property. Many people are willing to do that because bees are good for their gardens - and they might get some free honey out of the deal!

Consider the Terrain

One thing that first-time beekeepers don't often think about is that full honeycombs weigh a lot. You don't want to have to carry them for long distances across rough terrain. So, it's important to place them as close to the harvesting area as possible.

If that isn't an option, you should at least make sure that you can get to and from the hive either with a wagon, cart, or preferably in a motorized vehicle. Just remember that the noise of a motor could aggravate the hive. So, bring the vehicle to a nearby location, but not right up to the hive.

Once you have harvested the honeycomb, you'll only need to carry it a short distance to the wagon or vehicle you then can easily transport it to and from the honey extraction area. That will help prevent pulling a muscle or putting your back out trying to carry all of the honeycombs on foot.

Raise Your Hives off the Ground

It's best to put your bee hives up on a few bricks or otherwise raise them a few inches off the ground. That will keep them from freezing, flooding or being invaded by ground insects or small animals. Many hives are accidentally killed off by improper drainage or air flow under the hive.

Hide Your Hives

It is strongly suggested that you hide your hives from prying eyes. It's a safe bet that your neighbors love honey, but hate getting stung by bees. As a beekeeper, you have a lot of control over the flight paths that your bees will take, but your neighbors don't know that. They may not be willing to listen to reason. In fact, if any bee stings them at all they might assume that it was one of your bees.

It's not just your neighbors that you need to secure your hives from. Depending on where you live, you may have animals in the area that like honey, such as raccoons or bears. So, it's best to place your apiary in a fenced in area or someplace that wildlife is unlikely to invade. The last thing you want is to wake up and find your hive destroyed.

Also, remember that fences won't always be enough to keep certain animals out. You may need to install electric fences or use other means to keep your bees safe. Be creative and use your resources. Beekeeping clubs and the Internet can be great places to get ideas.

Create a Bee Haven

Create a bee haven on your own property, particularly if you want to keep your bees away from your neighbors. Have lots of flowering plants - be sure to plant a wide variety - and a decent shallow water source to encourage your bees to stay fairly close to home. Bees like having plants that flower at different times, to keep them well supplied with nectar and pollen.

Bees cannot fly when their wings get wet, so when you are creating a water source for your bees use leaves or other light floating objects to give them something to cling to. The goal is to help your bees collect water, not to drown them.

Control Flight Paths

Controlling the flight paths of your bees is also important. For a start, don't put the hive right next to your door or in an area where you, your family, your pets, or your neighbors frequently travel. Also, remember that bees tend to go straight up to avoid obstacles and then they often stay at that height until they see the flowers and plants that they want. Therefore, you can use a trellis, fence, or other tall objects to get your bees to go up and over anyplace that you don't want them.

Spread Out Your Hives

If you are planning to have two or more beehives, you should spread them out a bit. Hives that are too close together can confuse the bees and create a lot of problems. It's best to give each hive its own little area. Then you can observe each colony separately.

As you can see, it's not too difficult to give your bees the best possible location once you get started. If you need help, ask a local beekeeper or beekeeping club. Then you can get all the latest buzz and "bee" happy with your choice.

5

WHAT EQUIPMENT AND ACCESSORIES WILL I NEED?

If you want to be a beekeeper, you need to start by getting the right equipment for the job. So, let's break the list down into some easy components.

Manuals and References

You might not think that manuals and references count as beekeeping equipment, but they are essential. Even the most experienced beekeeper might need help from time to time. There is absolutely no shame in admitting that you don't know all about bees, whether you have been working with them for five minutes, five years or 50 years.

You can easily purchase books, consult a manual, or read articles on the Internet. However, it's also a good idea to join a local beekeeping club because fellow beekeepers can be great sources of information and advice. They may even have some equipment that you can borrow from time to time.

The Hives

After the reference materials, the first thing that any beekeeper needs to get is hives. How many you need depends on how many bees you want to keep. Beginners usually opt to start with just one or two hives. Remember that you always have the option of expanding later on.

There are many different types of hives to pick from. If you like do-it-yourself projects, you could even build your own hives. However, as a beginning beekeeper, you're probably better off just buying the hives that you need. You may be able to get them from another local beekeeper. If not, you can order them online.

The most popular type of modern beehive is a Langstroth hive, which contains frames that are easily removable to harvest honey or inspect the hive. Other hives are not as user-friendly as Langstroth hives.

Supers

If you decide to build your own hives, you'll also need supers, which are basically just honey storage containers that are usually positioned above the brood chamber. Langstroth hives come with built-in supers, which is another good reason to simply purchase a pre-assembled Langstroth hive.

A Hive Tool

A hive tool is also a critical piece of equipment for any beekeeper. It is an elongated metal hook used to pop open the hive covers for inspections. You'll also need your hive tool any time you want to add new boxes to a hive or harvest honey or wax from the hive.

If needed, a sharp knife and a crowbar are good substitutes for a hive tool. But if you buy two or three of them then you will always have a spare hive tool handy when you need it.

A Bee Brush

A bee brush is one of the most important tools for a beekeeper. Yet, it's one of the tools that beginning beekeepers often forget about. A bee brush is specially designed to gently sweep bees off of the honey comb when you are trying to harvest it. You can use your bee brush to direct your bees to and from certain areas. However, be careful because your bees are not going to like being swept aside.

A Smoker

There is no way that you can be a beekeeper without a smoker, which relaxes the bees into a manageable state so that you can harvest honey from the hive. The smoker can also be handy when you are setting up the hive, inspecting it, expanding it, and doing several other tasks related to your beekeeping.

The interesting thing about a smoker is that it doesn't just put bees "to sleep." It causes them to eat a lot of honey. They stock up because they expect an impending fire. Smoking the hive can also interfere with the way in which the bees communicate with each other. That means that they are less likely to stage a full scale assault on you while you are tending to the hive.

A Bee Suit

One of the first things people think of when they think of beekeeping is the bee suit, which consists of a jacket, gloves, and a veil. A bee suit is usually tan or white and, hopefully, bee proof. If you are an especially nervous person, you'll definitely want a bee suit.

The important thing to remember about bee suits is that they aren't perfect. So, it will be up to you to make sure to take a few added precautions. For example, you may want to tape or pin your pants in such a way that the bees cannot crawl in and climb up your legs. You should do the same with the areas where your gloves meet your arms.

Harvesting Equipment

Other than the bees themselves, those are the basic pieces of equipment that you will need to start with. However, if you plan to harvest honey and wax from your bees then you will need some other items, including:

o A shed or shack where you can harvest the honey
o A honey extractor (separator)
o A wagon or other method of transporting the honey supers to and from the shed
o An uncapping tray
o A settling tank
o Filters
o Food grade, air-tight buckets or jars to store the extracted honey
o Labels for the honey jars

Although that covers most of the starting equipment that you'll need, there are other items you may want to get later. For example, you may find yourself needing feeders, queen cages, queen marking pens, and other odds and ends. Again, your local bee club can be a great source of information. You can also purchase pre-made beekeeping starter kits online. Just remember to always "bee" alert because you never know when your bees might need something that you initially forgot.

6

WHAT KIND OF BEE WILL BE IN MY HIVE?

There are around 20,000 bee species in the world, but not all of them are suitable for beekeeping.

Bee Species

Ground bees aren't usually good for beekeeping since they can create hives in dangerous places and aren't known for their honey or wax production. Another common type of bee is the bumblebee. Bumblebees are very cute at a distance and they are also fairly harmless. It takes a lot to make a bumblebee angry. So, it's fairly safe to have bumblebees around. Also, their big fuzzy bodies make them great pollinators, which makes gardeners love them. Unfortunately, most beekeepers are out to harvest wax and honey and bumblebees are not suitable for such purpose, because the amounts they produce are minimal.

As a beekeeper, therefore, you probably want to keep some sort of honey bee in your hives. The exact type of honey bee, however, is going to depend on what area you live in and what it is that you are specifically looking for.

Here are some options:

Italian Honey Bees

Italian honey bees are probably the most common species kept by beekeepers. They are great for beginners because they tend not to swarm and they are fairly gentle. They're also excellent honey producers. The only big problems are that they require a lot of food in winter because they tend to create large colonies, which have been known to raid other hives when food is scarce.

Caucasian Honey Bees

Caucasian honey bees are slow to start up in the spring, but they tend to have a strong, large population. They also have better access to food sources, because they will forage on cool days and start foraging earlier in the day. They can be a bit problematic for new beekeepers because while generally calm, they don't calm back down easily once they are upset.

Carnolian Honey Bees

Carnolian honey bees can be a great choice for beginning beekeepers because they are extremely gentle. They produce great honey comb and start up easily in the spring. They also don't require that much food to sustain them through the winter. The only problem is that they are prone to swarming and splitting off into new hives. So, as the beekeeper, you really need to keep a close eye on them.

Russian Honey Bees

Russian honey bees are a good choice for some established beekeepers in certain parts of the world. They are resistant to a lot of different mites and problems. They can also deal well with colder winters. However, they can be very expensive! So, they are not great starter bees.

Invading Bees

Occasionally, you might also see invading bees go into your hive. That generally happens when a nearby hive swarms, splitting into two groups, and looks for nesting areas or if they have a food shortage and want to steal your hive's honey.

The workers can generally repel invading bees but you might need to step in. So, if you notice any suspicious hive activity, "bee" on the alert and you'll do fine.

Frank Randall

7

HOW DO I MANAGE MY HONEYBEE COLONY?

If you are just starting out as a beekeeper, you probably want to know how best to manage your bee colony. The short answer is that you shouldn't try to, unless you have to! Bees are fairly self-sustaining and too much interference can actually harm the hive.

Nevertheless, there are times when a beekeeper needs to manage the hive, and it's important to be prepared for when that happens. Here is a brief rundown of instances when you may need to manage your hive:

Inspections

It's important to periodically inspect your honeybee hive to identify possible problems within the hive. For example, you can look to see if the hive has mites, is experiencing a food shortage, or is otherwise compromised in some way.

Cluster Management

One example of a potential hive problem is clustering. Occasionally bees will cluster together in a certain area of the hive, especially in the winter to stay warm. Unfortunately, the clusters can sometimes move away from the food stores. If that happens, you will have to manage your hive by moving the honeycombs that are full nearer to the bee cluster.

Adjusting for Hive Size

The time may come when you need to manage your hive by adjusting its size to give the bees additional space. A more likely scenario is that you may need to simply split the bees into two hives.

If you do need to divide your honey bee hive in two, you'll need to move comb and capped honey, stored pollen, some new egg cells, and capped brood cells from the parent hive to the offspring hive. You will also need to transfer some of the worker bees to the new hive. The workers will then raise a new queen, drones, and more workers and your second hive will soon be in good shape.

Just remember that two hives should never be too close together. It's important to place your offspring hive a good distance away from your parent hive.

Transporting the Colony

In many areas, it's quite common to transport an entire bee colony for the purpose of pollination. Someone might actually hire you to bring your bees to their property to pollinate their crops.

The best time to move a hive, for any reason, is at night when bees are generally calmer. Remember to block any entrances and exits before moving the hive and remember to unblock them at your destination. Also, be sure to wear the right protective gear and keep your smoker handy, just in case of any problems.

Harvesting Honey and Wax

One of the most important times to actively manage your honey bee hive is when harvesting the honey and wax. You can easily recognize when it's harvest time because your bees will become aggressive. Also, you may see large numbers of worker bees outside the hive.

Before you harvest the honey, be sure to put on your protective clothing and smoke the hive. Then wait a couple of minutes for the bees to settle down. After that you can begin the process of honey harvesting - just remember to leave enough honey for the bees.

Timing

The timing of when to actively manage your honey bee colony will depend a lot on the type of honey bee and where in the world you live. In general, however, there is a certain calendar of events. January is usually the time you plan for the new season. That could include building new hives and ordering supplies. February and March are the months where you should really keep a close watch to see that your bees have enough food and are not in any danger.

Later in the year, generally April through June, make sure that your bees have what they need to make ample honey stores. That means giving them food, water, and space. You may also need to install more supers (honey storage containers).

Then, through July, August and possibly into September, is the time to extract honey.

During October and November, focus on getting your bees ready for the long winter. That could include feeding them, treating them for mites, ventilating the hive, securing it for the winter, and other related tasks.

December is usually an off month for a beekeeper, but that doesn't mean you can't plan ahead. A big part of hive management is anticipating what is coming up, and learning how to deal with problems before they arrive. So become active in local bee clubs and read plenty of magazines and articles. Also, take the time to replace any old equipment and make sure that you'll have everything that you need ready for the new season.

Things to Remember about Managing Your Hive

Finally, there are two significant things to remember about managing your beehive. First, you act as your hive's second line of defense.

They can manage themselves fairly well, but they might need your help sometimes. So, take an active role. Get to know your hive so that you can easily spot problems, such as mites, and treat them quickly.

Second, remember that you and your bees should learn how to co-exist and "bee" happy together. It's a mutually beneficial relationship, after all. So, you should do your best to only harvest what you need from the hive. See to it that your bees have enough left over to sustain the hive until next season. That will help to preserve and protect the bee population as well as save you from always having to start fresh each season.

8

HOW AND WHEN TO HARVEST HONEY

There are a lot of great things about being a beekeeper. One of the best is that you get to harvest your own honey. However, the harvesting process is not always easy. One of the tougher aspects, especially for a new beekeeper, is knowing when to harvest.

Wait a Season

You should not go into beekeeping expecting to have jars and jars of honey stocked up within a few months. A new colony needs time to build up and strengthen so you shouldn't harvest any honey at all from your hives during the first honey season. Your bees will need it all to survive the winter.

It can be a long wait for that first honey harvest, especially if you have a taste for honey; just remember that patience will definitely be rewarded.

Wait for the Nectar Flow

Once your hive is large enough and strong enough, wait for the nectar flow. Bees need nectar in order to make honey so when the flowers start to bloom, you should see things start to happen within the hive. After the nectar flow, inspect the hive to see what kind of progress your bees are making.

Recognize Harvest Time Behavior

You don't have to rely solely on a calendar or a blooming flower to tell when harvest time is at hand. The worker bees will tell you, too, by becoming extremely aggressive and stinging easily. You'll also see many more workers outside, either harvesting or defending the hive. So, if your ordinarily docile hive suddenly turns on you, it's reasonable to infer there may be some honey in there that to them is worth protecting. To you, it's probably worth harvesting.

Do Not Wait Too Long

One thing to keep in mind is that there can be multiple nectar flows in a season. After the last big one, your honey is going to be at risk for two reasons. First, the weather could turn and cold honey doesn't flow well, and is nearly impossible to extract. It can become granulated and thick. That means that you will have lost out on your harvest.

Another problem with waiting too long is that your bees will definitely be able to sense when winter is coming. That will cause them to eat a lot of honey in preparation. They may also move some honey out of the supers and into cells lower down in the hive. This is much the same as squirrels and small animals storing nuts for the winter. If that happens and you decide to harvest the supers, you'll find them almost empty.

Recognizing Harvest-Ready Honeycomb

A honeycomb is harvest ready when it's at least 80 percent sealed off, or capped. Whether to harvest then, or wait until it is completely full is entirely up to you. Just don't wait too long or you could miss out.

Also, it's important to remember to harvest honey without killing the bees. They are going to need a decent supply of honey for the winter so be sure to calculate what they need and leave enough to sustain them. You may also have to feed your bees or perform some maintenance on the hive leading up to winter ensuring they will survive.

The Harvesting Process

For the harvesting process you will need the following:

o A hive tool or alternate way to open the hive
o Protective clothing
o A wagon or way to transport the supers to the extraction area
o An extraction area (generally a heated shed)
o A knife and a bee brush
o A food grade bucket with a lid
o An extraction device
o Jars, pens, and labels
o A smoker

Simply smoke the hive and wait for two or three minutes. Be sure not to over-smoke it. A couple of puffs should do. Then open the hive and remove the combs using your hive tool, knife, and bee brush as needed. Then transport the combs to the extraction area.

Once again using your knife, scrape the caps off the honeycombs and then place each frame in the extractor to get the honey out of the combs. Then, after placing a strainer-covered bucket under the spigot, open it to allow the honey to flow out of the extractor, through the strainer, and into the bucket.

Once the honey is in the bucket, discard any excess wax or debris that was caught by the strainer. Now you will be ready to move the honey into canning jars. Be careful to label each jar, and then you can use it or sell it as you wish.

A Word of Caution

Even the most docile of bees can get riled up when their honey is being stolen, so always keep your protective gear on and your smoker handy during the honey harvesting process. It's also a good idea to make sure that you are extracting the honey in a sealed room that is a good distance from any hives. That way you won't have too many of that hive's bees chasing after you, and it'll reduce the risk of other area bees or animals coming after the honey as well.

Harvesting honey isn't an exact process. It is different in each part of the world and with each type of honey bee, so you need to get to know your own hives. If you are a patient, careful, and observant beekeeper, you shouldn't have any trouble figuring out when to harvest and how much to leave for the bees. All you have to do is "bee" aware of how your bees are acting and react to them accordingly.

9

WHAT EFFECT ON POLLINATION DO MY BEES HAVE?

If you want to keep bees in order to pollinate crops, here are some things that you should know.

The Process

The process of pollination is a simple one. The male part of the plant, the stamen, makes pollen, which is used to fertilize the stigma, the top portion of the pistil, or female plant part. This is a process that has been going on for thousands of years in some form or another, but not without help.

Unlike humans or animals, most plants can't reproduce at will on their own. The stamen can produce pollen, but that pollen has to be moved to the pistil. Water and wind are two ways in which pollen can be transferred; birds, animals, and insects are another.

Pollination in Farming

When it comes to pollination and its use in farming, wind, water, birds and large animals are virtually useless. They may do some pollinating, whether farmers want them to or not, but they aren't reliable. A farmer's crops cannot wait for days or weeks for a windy day. Nor can farmers train birds or animals to rub against a plant and then move to another and pollinate it.

So, Why Do Bees Pollinate Willingly?

As with any other work, bee pollination is done for one reason and one reason only: the bees get rewarded for their efforts. In this case, the payoff is nectar, which the bees use to make honey.

In fact, bees are so attracted to nectar, which is a mixture of water and sugar, they find flowers with high levels irresistible. In the process of harvesting nectar, the pollen attaches itself to their hairy bodies. Then, as the bee moves from plant to plant, pollination takes place.

Directing the Bees

Admittedly, bees can't really be trained to pollinate. Science hasn't developed that far yet. However, there are plenty of ways to direct the bees. For example, worker bees tend to travel about one to two miles (three kilometers) from their hive. So, farmers can set up a hive within that range of their crops.

Bees also tend to travel up to get around obstacles. So, trees and other objects can often be used to sort of guide the flight path of the bees. In that way, farmers and beekeepers can work together to direct bees to pollinate crops.

Personal versus Professional Uses

The impact your bees can have on pollination depends on whether you are keeping them for personal or professional use. If you are keeping them just to make honey for you and your family, you may want to plant a garden. That will give your bees a food source and could also result in you getting some great flowers and vegetables in the bargain.

Having a personal garden can be cheaper and more convenient than buying all of your food at the grocery store. It also gives you a healthy alternative to some of the pesticide and additive-filled food sold in stores.

On the other hand, if you want to keep bees professionally, you may find it lucrative to rent your hives to area farmers during pollination periods. It's amazing how much pollination a few honeybee hives can handle in a short period of time. If you can make money, get honey, and do your part to help local farmers grow crops, that's a great way to both make a living and make your area and the world as a whole a better place.

A Helping Hand

Honeybees can also be great for pollinating areas that are a bit out of the way or subject to odd weather patterns. For example, the feral bees in the area may stay in hiding during cold weather, but certain honey bee types are more resilient. Also, you have the ability to bring your bees to a farm on a warm day when they are more active. Feral bees come and go as they please, which means that pollination may not take place. With a helping hand from your honeybees, plants and flowers that otherwise wouldn't have a chance can easily reproduce.

Fighting the Decrease in Pollination

Pollination, particularly in North America, has been experiencing a rapid decline over the last several years. Changing weather patterns and an increase in disorders and problems within bee colonies are to blame. In fact, Colony Collapse Disorder has caused several beekeepers to give up on the business of beekeeping entirely.

Yet, many beekeepers are stepping up to the challenge and doing anything they can to protect their hives. In so doing, they are protecting the delicate process of pollinating and preserving the future for everyone, including the honeybees.

If you want to do your part as a beekeeper to fight the decrease in pollination, you're in luck. There are plenty of ways that you can help, with even one hive of honeybees. If you have multiple hives, that's even better. All you have to do is transport them to different farms as needed. Just be sure to do so at night, when the bees are less active.

"Bee" Aware

As a beekeeper, you also need to "bee" aware of any pollination problems with your hives or in your general area. The best way to stay informed is to inspect your hive often. If it looks unhealthy, don't transport it to any local farms. In fact, it's best not to transport your bees too far out of your local home area, even if they appear to be healthy. Also, keep informed on the latest beekeeping news in your area. That way you will know quickly if there are any cases of viruses or hive-invading insects anywhere near your home.

10

WHAT DISEASES AND PESTS CAN HARM MY BEES?

Beekeeping can be quite an up and down business. It's fun to watch the progression of the hive; that is, until the hive becomes abandoned, infested, or otherwise affected by diseases and pests. Knowing which pests to watch for depends on a number of factors, including time of year, location, and age of the hive. Here are some diseases and pests to look out for.

Varroa Mites

These parasites have invaded most of the world, with the exception of Australia. Varroa mites feed off of bees in all their forms - adult, pupal, and larval - so, an invasion can be a real hazard to your hive. They were first discovered in Southeast Asia around 1904 and rapidly spread. They struck in the United States in 1987, the UK in 1992, and New Zealand in 2000, leaving a lot of dead and deformed bees in their wake.

Fortunately, some of the bee populations are starting to recover. However, regardless of what part of the world you live in, you need to be on the alert for these invasive pests. They can be treated chemically if they're caught early. However, you should be aware of the rules in your area regarding use of certain chemicals, such as thymol or coumaphos.

Acarine (Tracheal) Mites

Acarine, or tracheal, mites used to be called the Isle of Wight Disease, because that's where they were first identified. It wasn't until much later on that the disease was caused by a mite that crawled out of the trachea of the bee and then moved to another bee to lay eggs.

The Buckfast bee is resilient to acarine mites. Other bees can be treated using patties made of one part vegetable shortening and three to four parts powdered sugar. When the bees eat the sugar, the shortening gets on them, confusing the mites so that they can't identify the bees properly.

Nosema

Nosema is essentially the bee version of dysentery. If they are stuck in the hive all winter and unable to go on cleaning flights, they can become ill. The solution for nosema is to keep the hive well-ventilated, although, beekeepers can also choose to treat nosema with antibiotics.

Wax Moths

In moderate climates, wax moths are another common type of bee hive pests. They are not usually a problem for beekeepers in areas with cold winters, because they cannot survive the low temperatures. Wax moths don't attack the bees themselves, but feed on beeswax and can destroy honeycomb and wax stores, which can lead to hive damage or destruction.

Small Hive Beetle

The small hive beetle is another pest that can easily invade your hive. Its larvae can make the comb slimy, causing the bees to move out and search for a new home. Small hive beetles are originally from Africa but have spread to the United States and other parts of the world. Cooking oil-based traps tend to keep the beetle infestations from getting out of control.

Bacterial and Fungal Hive Infections

Aside from small insects, there are several regional bacterial and fungal infections that can take hold in a beehive, including:

o American Foulbrood
o European Foulbrood
o Stonebrood
o Chalkbrood

There are also a number of paralytic viruses that can infect a bee colony. Some of those include

o Chronic paralysis virus (CPV)
o Acute bee paralysis virus (ABPV/APV)
o Israel acute paralysis virus (IAPV)
o Kashmir bee virus (KPV)

Colony Collapse Disorder (CCD)

CCD is a disorder that isn't widely understood. First noticed in North America in 2006, it's a phenomenon where all of the worker bees disappear from a hive. Similar problems have been seen in Spain, Portugal, France, the Netherlands, Belgium, Germany, Taiwan, and a few other areas although it seems to be worst in North America.

Some studies suggest that Varroa and Acarine mites might contribute to Colony Collapse Disorder but so far there is no definitive proof. It is imperative that beekeepers be on the lookout for signs of the disorder and to be careful about transporting colonies that may be infected from one area to another.

Pesticide Contamination

Although it's not technically a pest or a disease, pesticide contamination is a huge problem for beekeepers. Some studies suggest there could be a connection between pesticides and Colony Collapse Disorder. Some bees travel one to two miles (up to three kilometers) in the process of gathering their nectar and pollen. That means that your bees may go onto properties that aren't yours.

There are a few things you can do to prevent pesticide contamination, including:

- o Do not use any pesticides on your property.
- o Plant gardens on your property to encourage bees to stay close to home.
- o Only keep bees in an area where they have plenty of room to roam and still stay on your property.
- o Ask your neighbors not to use pesticides on their properties to help preserve the healthy bee population.

As you can see, there are a lot of risks involved in being a beekeeper. However, there are also a lot of rewards, including doing your part to preserve the bee population. Just be sure to inspect your hives and stay informed on the latest bee care tips, especially if those tips involve natural methods.

CONCLUSION

I hope this book has given you an insight into beekeeping and helped make up your mind whether it's for you.

Although I have done my best to summarize the subject for this little introductory book, apiculture is complicated and very involving even on the smallest scale. But it is incredibly rewarding and can be a unique part of your life, as well as beneficial to the environment both locally and globally.

Oh, and eating the honey from your own hive is rather wonderful too!

Best wishes,

Frank Randall

Ohio
September 2012

USEFUL RESOURCES

Beekeeping Clubs

A frequently updated list of clubs located worldwide.

backyardfarmbooks.com/clubs

Beekeeping Magazines

americanbeejournal.com

beeculture.com

Advanced Beekeeping Books

Natural Beekeeping: Organic Approaches to Modern Apiculture by Ross Conrad - backyardfarmbooks.com/NB

The Practical Beekeeper Volume I, II & III Beekeeping Naturally by Michael Bush - backyardfarmbooks.com/PB

Beehive Starter Kits

These are ideal for beginners, and much cheaper than buying all the tools and accessories you need separately.

CoolMax Polystyrene Bee Hive Kit - backyardfarmbooks.com/CM

Standard Bee Hive Kit backyardfarmbooks.com/SB

Complete Bee Hive Kit with Bee Suit - backyardfarmbooks.com/CB

Gold Standard Bee Hive Kit - backyardfarmbooks.com/GS

Frank Randall

ABOUT THE AUTHOR

Frank was born and bred in Bradford, West Yorkshire, England, in 1945. Born into a family of mill workers, he spent much of his free time on the Yorkshire Moors feeding his fascination with wildlife and nature. He later went on to lecture at the BICC. In 1995 he immigrated to the USA and now lives in peace on the shores of Lake Erie, Ohio, with his wife, two dogs, a colony of honeybees, and a menagerie of other critters.

He's the author of Amazon's #1 Best Selling Backyard Farm Books, which include *The Bee Book for Beginners*, *The Worm Book for Beginners*, and *The Mushroom Book for Beginners* and *The Sustainable Living Book for Beginners*.

@BackyardFarmBks
facebook.com/BackyardFarmBooks
backyardfarmbooks.com

Frank Randall

YOUR FREE GIFT

To get your copy just visit…

backyardfarmbooks.com/gobee

…and sign up for my free newsletter.

If you have a minute to leave a review of this book at Amazon that would be fantastic!

This URL will take you straight to the review page:

backyardfarmbooks.com/beereview

Frank Randall

ALSO FROM THIS AUTHOR

ALSO FROM THIS AUTHOR

Frank Randall

ALSO FROM THIS AUTHOR

Made in the USA
San Bernardino, CA
17 December 2013